Get Your Financial House in Order

Darlene C. Rivers
Rivers and Assoc. Inc
2nd Edition

© Copyright 2018 – Darlene C. Rivers

All rights reserved worldwide. This book is protected by the copyright laws of the United States of America. This book may not be copied or reprinted for commercial gain or profit.

Use of short quotations or occasional page copying for personal or group study is permitted and encouraged. Permission will be granted upon request. Remember to give proper credit for the information, and share the link to Rivers and Assoc. Inc's website www.RiversandAssoc.com.

Specific resources listed in this book have no connection with the author or publisher of this book. They are mentioned as examples. Names and links are provided so the readers may obtain information for themselves. Because of the dynamic nature of the Internet, any web addresses or links contained in this book may have changed since publication and may no longer be valid.

Publisher:
DavonnePress, a Danico Enterprises Inc. venture
126 E. Wing St, #264
Arlington Heights, IL 60004

Editor: DavonnePress

Disclaimer:
The views expressed in this work are solely those of the author and do not necessarily reflect the views of the publisher, and the publisher hereby disclaims any responsibility for them. This book is for informational purposes only.
The author and publisher do not accept any responsibilities for any liabilities resulting from the use of this information. While every attempt has been made to verify the information provided here, the author and the publisher cannot assume any responsibility for errors, inaccuracies or omissions.

ISBN-13: 978-1548354473
ISBN-10: 1548354473

Table of Contents

Forward — 1

Chapter 1 - Money — 5
Definition — 5
Who Do Men Say That I Am? — 5
Hindrances — 6
Negative Talk — 8
God's Plan for Your Finances — 9
Applying Principles for Life to Money — 10
Next Step — 11

Chapter 2 - Budget — 13
Definition — 13
Determine Where Your Money Goes — 13
Evaluate Income vs. Expense — 18
How to Allocate Your Funds — 20
Create a Budget — 21
Next Step — 28

Chapter 3 - Net Worth — 29
Definition — 29
How Does God Calculate Net Worth? — 29
Determining Natural Net Worth — 29
Determining Your New Net Worth — 32
Next Step — 37

Chapter 4 - Estate Planning — 39
Definition — 39
Letter of Intent — 40
Beneficiary Designations — 40
Durable Power Of Attorney (POA) — 40
Healthcare Power of Attorney (POA) — 41
Last Will and Testament — 41
Living Trusts — 42
Guardianship Designations — 43
Critical Mishaps When Estate Planning — 44
Next Step — 48

Chapter 5 - Retirement   49
Definition   49
What the Bible Says About Retirement   50
What Should Retirement Look Like?   51
Retirement Planning   51
Does Retirement Planning Take Time?   55
Is It Too Late to Plan for Retirement?   55
Next Step   56

Epilogue   59
Principles for Life   60

About the Author   63

Resources   65

Forward

So why another book or lecture on money for Christians?

I believe my assignment is to help the household of faith. Simply put, I believe many Christians lack a biblical foundation for their finances. Many believers are trying to build an entire financial structure on one scripture (Malachi 3:10).

Malachi 3:10 KJV
Bring ye all the tithes into the storehouse, that there may be meat in mine house, and prove me now herewith, saith the Lord of hosts, if I will not open you the windows of heaven, and pour you out a blessing, that there shall not be room enough to receive it.

Malachi 3:10 is a great foundational scripture however it does not give your financial house walls, window or doors, nor does it teach you how to maintain what you have. Scriptures such as Proverbs 27:23 will help you build walls and doors for a strong financial home.

Proverbs 27:23 TLB
So watch your business interest closely, Know the state of your flocks and your herds;

There are over 155 verses about money in the Bible, but the church seems to struggle more than the world. The purpose of this book is to empower believers to create a firm financial foundation.

As individuals, you must first look at your attitude regarding money. Are you truly running your financial lives? Are you in charge? Is money your slave or your master? Have you come to an understanding that money in and of itself is simply a tool and it works for you? As the saying goes, you cannot change or confront what you do not acknowledge.

It is also wise to look at hindrances in your life. There are actual obstacles, which affect your financial life. For some it's as simple as lack of knowledge.

Hosea 4:6 KJV
My people are destroyed for lack of knowledge...

Your attitude towards money could be sabotaging you. For example, negative speak can be working in your subconscious.

A lack of integrity for the believer is a diffident hindrance. I point you to -

Proverbs 6:30-31 AMP
People do not despise a thief if he steals To satisfy himself when he is hungry; But when he is found, he must repay seven times [what he stole]; He must give all the property of his house [if necessary to meet his fine].

Lastly, perhaps you are being oppressed or overwhelmed and the idea of adding one more thing to an already busy list makes your head swim. *Been there. Relax. Stand on.*

Matthew 11:30 AMP
For My yoke is easy [to bear] and My burden is light

My job is to give you practical tools to enhance your life, not add more disorder. This book takes a glimpse at understanding money and some of the hindrances that may be holding back believers. The four building blocks that lead to a stable financial home will be the main focus:

- ☐ Budget
- ☐ Net Worth
- ☐ Estate Planning
- ☐ Retirement Planning

To gain total success on each building block you need to apply the following basic "Principles for Life":

- ☐ Understand the Problem
- ☐ Discuss with God
- ☐ Get Revelation (Word)
- ☐ Receive Instructions
- ☐ Follow the Instructions

We know according to (Hebrews 4:2) the gospel was preached; however, it didn't profit everyone because it was not mixed with faith. Do not separate your financial life from your Christian life. God has an individual plan for each and every one of you. But you're going to have to seek God for the Plan. You're going to have to ask God for the instructions.

Chapter 1
Money

Psalm 127:1-2 AMP
Unless the Lord builds the house, they labor in vain who build it; Unless the Lord guards the city, The watchman keeps awake in vain. It is vain for you to rise early, To retire late, To eat the bread of anxious labors— For He gives [blessings] to His beloved even in his sleep.

Definition

Money is often defined as a current medium of exchange in the form of coins and banknotes; (money printed on paper, constituting a central bank's promissory note to pay a stated sum to the bearer on demand)

When building any structure, you first need to understand what materials you'll need. You also must know the rules in your area regarding permits and zoning to build the structure. The same concept applies to your financial house. One raw material you will need at some point is money. You will have to exchange this money to get something else. Since we must exchange money for other goods and services it's appropriate that we stop and take a look at the impact it has.

Who Do Men Say That I Am?

This quote from Mark 8:27 really got me thinking what do we really think about money? Your attitude around money has a lot to do with how you handle it. Author, radio host, television personality, and owner of The Lampo Group, Inc., Dave Ramsey describes it in his YouVersion devotional this way - pretend you started a company called YOU Inc. and it's your job to manage every cent. If you manage money for YOU Inc. the way you manage money now would you be fired? Well, you are in charge of YOU Inc. You are responsible for managing the money God's entrusted to you which is even more important. Dave explains that money is active. It's always moving, always flowing from one thing to another. Money flows away from those who don't manage it and towards those who do manage it.

Pastor Rick Warren author and founder of Saddleback Church has a YouVersion devotional which teaches that money is either a slave or a master. It's a terrific servant and a lousy master. When money is your master you're always under stress. You're always worried. When you're the master of your money, it's your servant, money serves you. When money works for you instead of you working for your money, then you have peace.

I believe money is a tool; a raw material to be used as I see fit. When I think about money I equate it to my favorite tool, my wooden hammer. I have all kinds of tools, sanders, saws, at least 3 drills, but my wooden hammer is my favorite tool. My grandfather would laugh, because I thought I could solve all my problems with my hammer. By itself the hammer does nothing. It's the pressure I apply and the task I give it that make it powerful.

You must identify, acknowledge and understand your relationship with money. Is money like a tool, your favorite spice, slave or master? Are you always chasing it instead of it following you? Is money working for you and preparing a place for you to rest peacefully? Are you managing your servant called money? Remember it will flow from those not managing it to those who do. Lastly, have you given it too much power? Money will not work for you if you never instruct or guide it. It's a servant, a tool to be used. Who do you say money is?

Hindrances

There are often hindrances which can affect your financial house. Here are some of the more common ones:

- [ ] **Lack of knowledge**
  As the saying goes you don't know what you don't know. Hosea 4:6 KJV speaks to the people being destroyed for lack of knowledge. If you're reading this book you're working on solving this hindrance.

- [ ] **Under attack**
  There are times when you may actually be under attack and oppression sets in. You become preoccupied with the problem and not the solution. You've accepted a yoke that

was not meant for you. You cannot move forward if you're on the defensive.

Psalm 9:9 AMP
The LORD also will be refuge and a stronghold for the oppressed, a refuge in times of trouble;

When facing what seems like insurmountable financial issues it's easy to feel overwhelmed and helpless, especially if you've been dealing with the problem for a while. Proverbs 13:12, says, "Hope deferred makes the heart sick". But again, this is a defensive posture. Hebrews 10:23 AMP says, "hold tightly to the confession of our hope without wavering, for He who promised is reliable and trustworthy and faithful (to His word)". Be careful not to allow a lack of money or resources to affect your spirit.

☐ **Lack of integrity**
It's sad to say, but many followers in the body of Christ lack integrity. Theft is a common problem. Believers show up late for work but clock in on time. They have stolen cable, bootleg movies, and have been known to write bad checks. Understand I'm speaking of intentional theft. Say you picked up a pen at work and absent-mindedly put it in your purse. I think you'll be okay, that's unintentional; just return the pen. But when I hear of believers claiming someone else's child on their taxes, well that's just simply theft. There's a cost for lack of integrity and theft. Proverbs 6:30-31 AMP talks about stealing, but it says when the theft is found, he must repay seven times. So I did some simple math. Earned income credit in 2017 per child was $1,500. Now you realize it's not cash just a credit that reduces your taxable amount. I digress, 7 X $1,500 is $10,500. Remember the scripture says when the theft is found you now owe in the Spirit $10,500. Now suppose you gave an offering say $100 at 100-fold that's only $10,000, your $500 short. There will always be an opportunity to steal but you really need to consider the cost.

☐ **Rebellion**
Are you a procrastinator or are you in rebellion? This

Get Your Financial House In Order, 2nd Edition

hindrance creeps in masking as something else. It's never obvious. Sometime our procrastination is our polite way of saying no to the plans of God. Then we find ourselves in lack.

Psalm 68:6 AMP
God makes a home for the lonely; He leads the prisoners into prosperity. Only the stubborn and rebellious dwell in a parched land.

Negative Talk

One barrier to financial freedom may be the negative talk you have going on in your head. Unintentionally many, myself included, were indoctrinated with negative images around money and financial issues. Here are a few I hear often:

- ☐ Don't ask for too much. You don't want to be greedy.
- ☐ God loves the poor.
- ☐ It's my lot in life. You'll always have bills.
- ☐ There will always be poor people.

As well meant and intended these words have been planted and can hinder your financial and personal growth. When working on your financial house, keep an eye open to these hidden dream killers. A tool to uproot and remove this negative talk from our lives is the word of God. For example, if your dream killer is "Don't ask for too much. You don't want to be greedy"; confess (Deuteronomy 8:18). This will enable you to put the focus back where it belongs on God.

Deuteronomy 8:18 KJV
But thou shalt remember the Lord thy God: for it is he that giveth thee power to get wealth that he may establish his covenant which he share unto they fathers, as it is this day.

If greed and motive is a concern it's okay to ask God to search you. Apply Psalms 139:23 -

Psalm 139:23 NLT
Search me, O God, and know my heart; test me and know my anxious thoughts.

The believer who confesses, it's my lot in life, really says a lot about their relationship with the Creator. 3 John 1:2 says "Beloved, I wish above all things that thou mayest prosper and be in health, even as thy soul prospereth". That doesn't sound like you're portion in life is debt.

These dream killers often come from well-meaning people. When I first started talking about coming out of debt and living better my friends would often quote Matthew 26:11. In short it says the poor will always be around. My response was where did you see my name on that scripture? In fact, where did it say the believer was the poor? These friends had no idea they were impacting my dreams, they said what they were taught.

When you identify that negative voice in your head always look for the counterbalance in the word of God. When applying scripture, you need to apply it properly, so remember 2 Timothy 2:15 -

2 Timothy 2:15 AMP
Study and do your best to present yourself to God approved, a workman [test by trial] who has no reason to be ashamed, accurately handling and skillfully teaching the word of truth.

God's Plan for Your Finances
First, we need to settle the argument that God is your source and supplier. The very names of God speak to this point:

- ☐ **El-Shaddai** - The God Almighty of blessings. The Breasty One who nourishes and supplies, all bountiful and all sufficient.

- ☐ **Jehova-Jireh** - The one who sees my needs and provides for them.

- ☐ **Jehova-Rohi** - My Shepherd and I shall not want for any good or beneficial thing.

All you have to do is look in God's word for assurances. We know from James 1:17 he's a good father, and every perfect gift comes from him. 2 Timothy 2:13 AMP tells us he's faithful. We know he loves us by his word in Isaiah 54:10 NLT. And if we ever get confused about his plans for us we simply need to read 1 Corinthians 2:9 and Jeremiah 29:11.

Because God has a plan for your life, you do not have to depend on the kindness of others, you simply have to depend on him.

Applying Principles for Life to Money

Now you have all this information around money, attitudes about money and more scriptures than you wanted. Often, we hear the word but we fall back into old habits. We allow the negative talk to take over. Negative talk says, "I've been here too long to get out of this"; or, "I did this to myself and got what I deserved". Before you allow the dream killer to take hold, try applying the "Principles for Life":

- ☐ Understand the Problem
- ☐ Discuss with God
- ☐ Get Revelation (Word)
- ☐ Receive Instructions
- ☐ Follow the Instructions

This book is not about accumulating stuff and money. It's about living the scriptures. As you surrender more and more of your finances to God and begin to trust him more, you will see greater increase. Going from limited or no resources to debt free doesn't come over night. God will not force you into your wealthy place, you will have to work and trust God. Remember God has a tailored made financial plan for everyone. You just need to ask him for the plan.

Next Step

Before moving to the next step take a moment and really think about your relationship with money. If money has been your master in the past it's time to turn that around. Second, keep your eyes and ears open for those negative thoughts around your finances. Take those dream killers and start bringing them into captivity. The MSG Bible says it this way "We use our powerful God-tools for smashing warped philosophies, tearing down barriers erected against the truth of God, fitting every loose thought and emotion and impulse into the structure of life shaped by Christ." (2 Corinthians 10:5).

Stop the negative talk.

Chapter 2
Budget

Proverbs 27:23 AMP
Be diligent to know the condition of your flocks, And pay attention to your herds;

Definition

A budget is an estimate of income and expenditure for a set period of time. It is your financial plan and a forecast for accounts and statements. A budget is your starting place. Before you can create a budget, you must complete the following steps:

1. Determine Where Your Money Goes
2. Evaluate Income vs. Expense
3. Dissect Debt
4. Allocate Your Funds

Determine Where Your Money Goes

Before you do anything, you have to have a starting point. To build and secure your financial house you must know and understand how much money you have coming in and how much money you have going out. To get a clear picture you need to examine your income and spending for 6 months or at the very least 3 months minimum. Income and expenses can fluctuate but with 6 months of information you'll get a better picture of where you are. Even if you are living debt free you still should do this at least once a year.

Keep it simple. You may have a personal financial service such as online banking or personal financial software such as Mint, Quicken or LearnVest. Use the tools you already have available to you. Personal financial services and personal financial software can provide you with income and expense figures in minutes. If you use multiple accounts you'll have to pull information from all of your accounts to get an accurate representation. If your automated tool does not combine all the accounts, download the transactions into a spreadsheet. If you don't have an automated tool this exercise can be done with pen and paper.

Once you've determined the right tool for you, next document your income as well as expenses. When doing this exercise remember to include all the money you received, not just your pay. If you received a commission, bonus, rebate, child support, business expense, government assistance, retirement or disability you need to add it in. If you received cash you need to add it in. If you have no idea how much cash you receive you'll need to start tracking it. Again, make it easy on yourself. Carry a small notebook that fits in your pocket and jot down every dollar you get or spend.

When recording expenses every payment should be included and that includes babysitter money, movie money, gifts, tithes and offerings. If you spent it you need to track it. Make sure your document, if you're using paper and pen or a spreadsheet, includes categories. It is crucial for you to understand how much you're spending per category.

When using personal financial services or personal financial software simply choose the time frame you wish to investigate. If an item is missing a category the system will alert you so you can update your transactions. With a little manipulation, this task can be completed in minutes. Remember to include all your accounts in the analysis.

To be clear, tracking can be broken down into three levels: pen and paper, spreadsheets, and personal financial software or personal financial systems.

Level 1 tracking uses pen and paper. Here you write down all your income and expenses for three months. Think of it as the old fashion check registry only with categories. If you record the transactions in category order this will allow you to create the summary quickly. This is a good way to get your kids started. They will undoubtedly move this to a spreadsheet once they get the hang of it.

\multicolumn{6}{c}{**Level 1 Pen and Paper Tracking**}				
Date	**Description**	**Category**	**Withdrawal**	**Deposit**
mm/dd/yy	T.J. Max	Clothing	$100.00	
mm/dd/yy	Marshalls	Clothing	$100.00	
mm/dd/yy	Sears	Clothing	$50.00	
mm/dd/yy	"Just in case" funds	Emergency Fund	$70.00	
mm/dd/yy	Movies	Entertainment	$10.00	
mm/dd/yy	Concert	Entertainment	$80.00	
mm/dd/yy	Sporting Event	Entertainment	$50.00	
mm/dd/yy	Grocery Store	Food	$175.00	
mm/dd/yy	Grocery Store	Food	$175.00	
mm/dd/yy	Grocery Store	Food	$175.00	
mm/dd/yy	Grocery Store	Food	$175.00	
mm/dd/yy	Housing	Housing (Rent/Mortgage)	$1,050.00	
mm/dd/yy	Medical	Medical	$420.00	
mm/dd/yy	Salary	Salary		$1,750.00
mm/dd/yy	Salary	Salary		$1,750.00
mm/dd/yy	Savings	Savings	$100.00	
mm/dd/yy	Savings	Savings	$100.00	
mm/dd/yy	Savings	Savings	$150.00	
mm/dd/yy	Car Loan	Transportation	$270.00	
mm/dd/yy	Insurance	Transportation	$50.00	
mm/dd/yy	Metra	Transportation	$100.00	
			$3,400.00	$3,500.00

Summary		
Category	**Total**	**% of Income**
Salary	$3,500.00	
Housing (Rent/Mortgage)	$1,050.00	30%
Food	$700.00	20%
Clothing	$250.00	7%
Transportation	$420.00	12%
Medical	$420.00	12%
Savings	$350.00	10%
Entertainment	$140.00	4%
Emergency Fund	$70.00	2%
Other	$0.00	0%

Get Your Financial House In Order, 2nd Edition

Level 2 tracking is the use of spreadsheets. In the following example, I used a check register spreadsheet. You simply download your transactions from your bank to your spreadsheet. You may have to add categories. Do not be concerned with the balance since the objective is to see the totals by category and not to balance your checking account. This works well if you have more than one account.

Check Register

Total Income: $3,500.00
Total Expense: $3,400.00
Savings: $100.00

		Level 2 tracking with spreadsheets			
Date	Description	Category	Withdrawal	Deposit	Balance
	Beginning Balance				$ -
	Salary	Salary		$1,750	$1,750
	Grocery Store	Food	$175		$1,575
	Grocery Store	Food	$175		$1,400
	Grocery Store	Food	$175		$1,225
	Grocery Store	Food	$175		$1,050
	Salary	Salary		$1,750	$2,800
	T.J. Max	Clothing	$100		$2,700
	Marshalls	Clothing	$100		$2,600
	Sears	Clothing	$50		$2,550
	Housing	Housing (Rent/Mortgage)	$1,050		$1,500
	Car Loan	Transportation	$270		$1,230
	Medical	Medical	$420		$810
	Savings	Savings	$100		$710
	Insurance	Transportation	$50		$660
	"Just in case" funds	Emergency Fund	$70		$590
	Savings	Savings	$100		$490
	Savings	Savings	$150		$340
	Movies	Entertainment	$10		$330
	Concert	Entertainment	$80		$250
	Sporting Event	Entertainment	$50		$200
	Metra	Transportation	$100		$100
			$3,400	**$3,500**	**$100**

Summary		
Category	Total	% of Income
Salary	$3,500.00	
Housing (Rent/Mortgage)	$1,050.00	30%
Food	$700.00	20%
Clothing	$250.00	7%
Transportation	$420.00	12%
Medical	$420.00	12%
Savings	$350.00	10%
Entertainment	$140.00	4%
Emergency Fund	$70.00	2%
Other	$0.00	0%

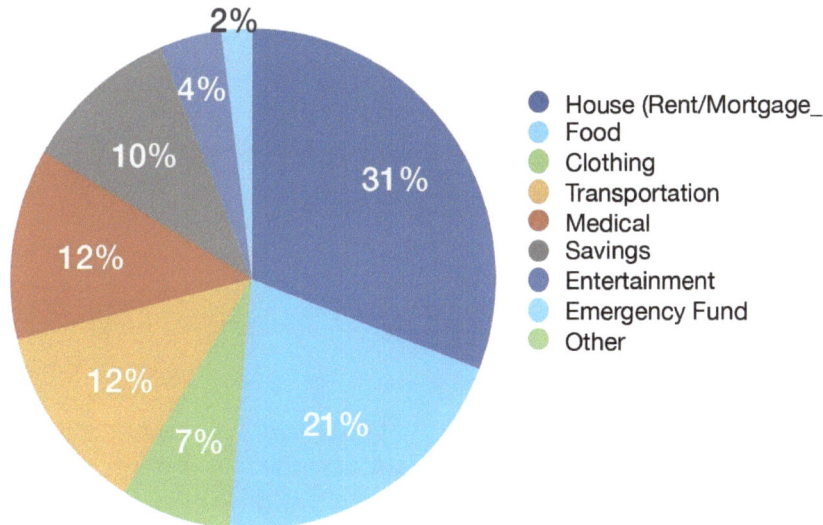

Personal financial software or personal financial systems are used in level 3 tracking. As in the case of using the online banking system here all the work is done for you. You simply input the dates you wish to use and a chart is provided showing percentage and amount spent per category. The system will also provide the list of transactions. Depending on the system you use there are additional reports you can create to assist you in understanding your financial situation.

Date	Payee	Category	Amount
1/14/2016	Savings	Savings	-100.00
1/5/2016	Concert	Entertainment	-80.00
1/5/2016	Grocery Store	Food & Dining	-175.00
1/5/2016	Housing	[Home Loan]	-1050.00
1/6/2016	Marshalls	Shopping: Clothing	-100.00
1/7/2016	Savings	Savings	-100.00
1/15/2016	Sears	Shopping: Clothing	-50.00
1/15/2016	Just In Case	Emergency Fund	-70.00
1/15/2016	Grocery Store	Food & Dining	-175.00
1/15/2016	Car Loan	Transportation	-270.00
1/16/2016	Medical	Medical	-420.00
1/17/2016	Grocery Store	Food & Dining	-175.00
1/21/2016	Savings	Savings	-150.00
1/24/2016	T.J. Max	Shopping: Clothing	-100.00

Before moving to the next step take a look at the data you've collected. Remember if you receive or spend cash you need to make sure it's accounted for.

Evaluate Income vs. Expense

So now you have 3 to 6 months' worth of data. Time to evaluate and understand the numbers.

Step 1. Calculate your average income

Take your 3 to 6 months of income and divide it by the number of months you used. Locating your income should be easy to find since you used the categories as suggested.

Step 2. Calculate your average monthly spend

Take your 3 to 6 months of spending and divide it by the number of months you used to get your monthly average spend.

Step 3. Calculate your average income vs. average spend

Subtract your average monthly income from your average monthly spend. Simple, right? So, if your monthly income has an average of $4,400 and your spend average is $4,300, your difference or savings is $100.00.

If your income is greater than your spending you have savings. If, however, you end up with a negative number you're spending more than you make and that's a problem.

The objective of the evaluation is to determine your financial health, no judgment. So now you know if you're spending more than you make. This is not the stopping point. The first principle from our "Principles for Life" says understand the problem. This is the same if your net balance is positive or a negative. Just because you have money at the end of the month doesn't mean you're done.

Dissect Your Debt
If you pulled your income and expense, numbers you probably already started this step. You started thinking why one category had a larger percentage than another. You started remembering what transactions made up these numbers and started to evaluate if you needed the things or goods and services. That's all that dissecting means. In this step, you want to take a closer look at what you're spending and ask the following questions:

1. Was it a Need (N) or a Want (W)? Could you have done without?

2. Does it have value (Y/N)? Meaning once it's paid off does it have a value? For example, a mortgage would be an item that is a need and also at the end of it you have a home so it brings you value. However, a student loan may be a need, but you're not going to get any additional value once it's paid off. Thus, it has no monetary value.

3. Can I reduce this category in the future? (Y/N/Maybe). For example, a cell phone could be considered a utility and if you find a lower plan, you could bring the cost down.

The answers to these questions are based your beliefs. There is no hard and fast rule. If you believe a student loan has value once paid off because you have a degree which can increase your earning mark value as yes. You are CEO of your finances so you have final say.

Using the information from the personal financial services example you can create a quick chart.

Category	Total Amount	%	Need/Want	Value (Y/N)	Reduce?
Housing (Rent/Mortgage)	$1,050.00	30%	N	Y	Maybe
Food	$700.00	20%	N	N	Yes
Clothing	$250.00	7%	W	N	Yes
Transportation	$420.00	12%	N	Y	Maybe
Medical	$420.00	12%	N	N	No
Savings	$350.00	10%	N	Y	Yes
Entertainment	$140.00	4%	W	N	Yes
Emergency Fund	$70.00	2%	N	Y	Yes
Other	$0.00	0%	N/A	N/A	N/A

Now that you've done your evaluation you can answer some real simple questions:

- ☐ Is it a spending issue? You just had to have that handbag?

- ☐ Is it a discipline issue? You started great and you're not sure how you got off track?

- ☐ Or is it an earnings issue? The ugly truth is for some people you simply don't have enough money to meet your day-to day needs.

Answering these questions will help you when adjusting your budget.

How to Allocate Your Funds

Determine what goes where. Now that you understand funds coming in and funds going out it's important to allocate your resources properly. As believers, the proper order is:

- ☐ Giving Tithes and Offering – Kingdom Business
- ☐ Personal Responsibility - Pay your bills
- ☐ Long Term Goals – (here's where you invest) Education, Retirement, Car, Home
- ☐ Me Time (you're last)

Before you toss this book in the trash I want to tell you, you're not going to find a financial resource or book that does not include these four items. They may not be in the same order or using the same terms but they're there. This order is for believers. As Christians, we put Kingdom Business first, which is your tithes and offerings. When you look at other advisors they simply call this philanthropy or charity, and you may find it lower on the list. Your second priority is paying your debts. As believers, we are to walk in integrity. That includes paying our bills on time. Third on the list is long term goals. This is a large category and includes savings, education for you and your children, retirement, your home, your car, emergency fund and investing. Last on the list is paying you. People ask all the time "should I pay me first"? No. There's been a misunderstanding when it comes to paying you first. I believe advisors meant that to mean contributing to savings, retirement, emergency fund, investments not vacations or expensive electronics. When I speak of "me time" I'm advocating paying yourself. It's the ability to purchase what you want without having any difficulty or shortfalls. Take the vacation knowing everything is accounted for so you can truly relax. Do not take the vacation if you're wondering how you're going to pay the electric bill when you return.

All of these steps are achievable. You must be committed to your success as God is committed to you.

Create a Budget
I hear groans every time I tell people to create a budget. Creating a budget is not a punishment! Creating a budget says you're making a conscious decision about your future and the future of your family. A budget says you have prioritized what's important to you and you have a plan. Put an end to sleepless nights and remove any unknown variables, develop a budget and get things under your control so you can breathe.

Mechanics
If you're using a spreadsheet there are numerous free budget spreadsheets. Do not recreate the wheel when doing your budget. All personal financial software or personal financial systems come with a budget plan.

If you've done any of the work outlined in this chapter you have the information needed to create a budget that will work for you. You've determined which tools work best for you. You've identified how much you have coming in and where your money is going. You've taken a look at your debt and now can determine a want from a need. You now can decide what steps are required to reduce or cancel debt. Understand this may necessitate a shift in your behavior. Focus on the behavioral changes which will give you the greatest impact instead of using a method of trial and error.

You just read how you should be spending your money and in what order. With the information you've collected, you can now set goals and come up with a proper plan. All of these steps constitute a personalized budget.

Budgets at the simplest level includes:

- Income - Money received, especially on a regular basis, for work or through investments.

- Fixed expenses - These are bills and expenses that don't vary much from month to month, like rent or mortgage payments, utilities and car payments. You may wish to add any bill with a fixed amount that you are committed to paying each month. Some people include gym memberships.

- Variable expense – These are day to day expenses such as food, hobbies, and gas.

Here are some examples:

	Level 1 Budgeting with pen and paper		
		Month CCYY	
	Budget	Actual	Difference
Personal Income			
Checking Balance	$100.00		
Income (salary, interest, tips)	$3,500.00		
Total Income	$3,600.00		
Fixed Expense			
Housing (Rent/Mortgage)	$1,050.00		
Transportation	$420.00		
Medical	$420.00		
Total Fixed Expense	$1,890.00		
Variable Expense			
Food (Grocery, Restaurants)	$700.00		
Clothing	$250.00		
Entertainment	$140.00		
Debt Payoff (minimum)	$100.00		
Savings	$350.00		
Emergency Fund	$70.00		
Other	$0.00		
Total Variable Expense	$ 1,510.00		
Total	$100.00		

Get Your Financial House In Order, 2nd Edition

Level 2 Budgeting with use of spreadsheets example 2

FAMILY BUDGET	YEAR:		
CASH AVAILABLE	**Month 1**	**Month 2**	**YTD TOTAL**
Monthly Cash	$100.00	$0.00	($2,693.00)
INCOME TYPE	**Month 1**	**Month 2**	**YTD TOTAL**
Income 1	$3,500.00	$3,500.00	$39,207.00
Checking Balance	$100.00		$100.00
TOTAL INCOME	**$3,600.00**	**$3,500.00**	**$39,307.00**
EXPENSES	**Month 1**	**Month 2**	**YTD TOTAL**
Housing (Rent/Mortgage)	$1,050.00	$1,050.00	$12,600.00
Transportation	$420.00	$420.00	$5,040.00
Medical	$420.00	$420.00	$5,040.00
Food (Grocery, Restaurants)	$700.00	$700.00	$8,400.00
Clothing	$250.00	$250.00	$3,000.00
Entertainment	$140.00	$140.00	$1,680.00
Debt Payoff (minimum)	$100.00	$100.00	$1,200.00
Savings	$350.00	$350.00	$4,200.00
Emergency Fund	$70.00	$70.00	$840.00
Other	$0.00	$0.00	$0.00
TOTAL EXPENSES	**$3,500.00**	**$3,500.00**	**$42,000.00**

Level 3 Budgeting with personal financial software or personal financial systems.

		Jan BUDGET	Feb BUDGET	Mar BUDGET	Apr BUDGET	May BUDGET	Jun BUDGET	Jul BUDGET	Aug BUDGET	Sep BUDGET	Oct BUDGET	Nov BUDGET	Dec BUDGET	2016 Summary BUDGET
▼ PERSONAL INCOME		3,500	0	0	0	0	0	0	0	0	0	0	0	3,500
	Net Salary	3,500	0	0	0	0	0	0	0	0	0	0	0	3,500
▼ PERSONAL EXPENSES		1,060	0	0	0	0	0	0	0	0	0	0	0	1,060
	Auto & Transport: Auto Insurance	0	0	0	0	0	0	0	0	0	0	0	0	0
	Auto & Transport: Auto Payment	0	0	0	0	0	0	0	0	0	0	0	0	0
	Auto & Transport: Transportation	0	0	0	0	0	0	0	0	0	0	0	0	0
	Bills & Utilities	0	0	0	0	0	0	0	0	0	0	0	0	0
	Deposit to Savings	0	0	0	0	0	0	0	0	0	0	0	0	0
	Entertainment	140	0	0	0	0	0	0	0	0	0	0	0	140
	Food & Dining: Groceries	0	0	0	0	0	0	0	0	0	0	0	0	0
	Health & Fitness	0	0	0	0	0	0	0	0	0	0	0	0	0
	Home: Mortgage	0	0	0	0	0	0	0	0	0	0	0	0	0

There is no hard and fast budgeting rule on how to distribute income and the percentage of distribution. There are a lot of variables to consider when it comes to budgeting like where you live and the size of your family. For example, a family of three in Kansas City, Missouri probably won't spend the same amount of money on groceries as a family of five in Los Angeles, California.

There are many general benchmarks; here are a few:

☐ LearnVest 50/20/30

Category	Percentages
Fixed Cost - These are bills and expenses that don't vary much from month to month, like rent or mortgage payments, utilities and car payments.	50%
Financial Goals - Paying down credit card debt, saving for retirement, and building an emergency fund.	20%
Flexible Spending – Day-to-day expenses that can vary from month to month, like eating out, groceries, shopping, hobbies, entertainment, or gas.	30%

☐ Elizabeth Warren, Harvard University bankruptcy expert and U.S. Senator, 50/30/20

Category	Percentages
Needs – Housing, utilities, transportation, etc.	50%
Wants -	20%
Debt repayment or planning for the future (retirement, savings, etc.)	30%

☐ Dave Ramsey – Author, radio host, television personality, and owner of The Lampo Group, Inc.

Category	Percentages
Charity	10-15%
Housing	25–35%
Utilities	5–10%
Food	5–15%
Transportation	10–15%
Medical Health	5–10%
Insurance	10–25%
Personal	5–10%
Recreation/Entertainment	5-10%
Savings	10-15%
Clothing	2-7%
Debt (goal 0%)	5-10%

☐ Everydollar.com

Category	Percentage
Giving	10-15%
Housing	25–35%
Utilities	5–10%
Food	10–15%
Transportation	10–15%
Health	5–10%
Insurance	10–25%
Personal	10-15%
Recreation	5-10%
Savings	10-15%

Here are some things often forgotten when planning a budget:

1. Savings - Saving money consistently is an important financial habit. The sooner you can build good financial habits the better off you will be. I want to emphasize saving isn't just about money, it's about a change of mindset. Your savings must have a purpose. If not, you will find your savings being spent. If your savings goes up and your debt goes up you really haven't saved anything. You only moved money around.

2. Plan for events – Christmas comes at the same time each year so you can plan for it. If you're hosting you can plan for the food and set money aside. Summer camp for your children should also be planned.

3. Maintenance – Home maintenance should be taken into account. Most experts advise that 1-3% of your home value should be set aside for maintenance. This would take care of the broken doorbell, kitchen faucet, and the plumber or any other maintenance worker that has to come out. Car maintenance should be budgeted. If your car is old you need to determine how much money you're going to put into the car and if it's time to start setting money aside for a new car.

4. Be flexible - A budget is a living thing and it changes. Periodically you will need to adjust your budget. A budget is not a punishment so don't remove all the fun and entertainment out of it. Just be more creative - use the library or Red Box instead of going to the movies. Do free festivals with your children instead of amusement parks. Take your own food to the amusement park if you go.

Remember money flows to those who manage it, so all items in your budget need a category. If you put everything under miscellaneous or savings don't be surprised if miscellaneous or savings seems to never be enough. Money as a servant has to have a job.

Proverb 23:5 NLT
In the blink of an eye wealth disappears, for it will sprout wings and fly away like an eagle

Next Step

Don't neglect to use the Principles for Life. To truly be successful you need to take the information you gathered here and discuss it with God, especially if you have more going out than you have coming in. Remember God's promise according to (3 John 1:2).

3 John 1:2 KJV
Beloved, I wish above all things that thou mayest prosper and be In health, even as thy soul prospereth.

Know what's happening with your money.

Chapter 3
Net Worth

Psalm 8:4-5 NLT
What are mere mortals that you should think about them, human beings that you should care for them? Yet you made them only a little lower than God and crowned them with glory and honor.

Definition

While the world defines your net worth as what you would have in cash if you sold every possession and paid off all of your debts. Your net worth is a barometer for measuring your financial health. Some people think net worth in relation to cash flow, worth, financial status, available means or lifestyle.

How Does God Calculate Net Worth?

It is important to understand that God does not use the basic definition for net worth when it comes to the believer. God does not look at your assets and assign a value to you as the world does. Throughout his word God places a value on his people, his children. A simple example is John 3:16, God gave his Son that we would not perish. In 2 Corinthians 5:21, God made him to be sin so we might be made the righteousness of God in him. Since we are made in God's image according to Genesis 1:26, we have the ability to define our natural net worth for we are to function like God. According to Job 22:28, it says decree a thing and it shall be established. Because you're working the "Principles for Life", discussing with God, and getting instructions you can be confident that what you're setting as net worth are within reach of God's plan for you. If you're only looking at your assets and liabilities to determine your net worth your math is wrong. There's much more to you than cash flow.

Determining Natural Net Worth

Using our "Principles for Life" we must first determine the problem or in this case where we are financially. You need to document your textbook net worth. Again, like your budget work, don't overthink it. A lot of the information you need you already have at your fingertips from the budget exercise. Here are some common categories that should be incorporated in your net worth document.

Asset	Debt
Real Estate	Mortgages
Home, Rental Property, Second Home, Other	Home mortgage payoff, Equity Credit Line, Other
Investments	**Personal Loans**
Stocks, Bonds, Savings Bonds, Retirement Account, Savings, CD, Mutual Funds, Cash Value of Life Insurance Policy	Car Loan, Personal Loas, Student Loans, Life Insurance Loans, Other
Personal Property	**Credit Cards**
Car, RV, Jewelry, Boat, Household Items, Other Luxury Goods	Credit Cards, Other Installment Loans
Cash	
Checking, Savings, Cash, Money Market, Other	

A net worth document can be done with simple pen and paper. There are many free templates available on the web as well as numerous free spreadsheets for personal net worth available on your computer.

I did a search on net worth calculation and in less than 5 minutes created a net worth spreadsheet using bankrate.com.

Assets		Liabilities	
Home	$1,000.00	Home mortgage principal	$1,000.00
Other real-estate	$1,000.00	Other mortgage principal	$0.00
Automobiles	$1,000.00	Auto loans	$1,000.00
Other vehicles	$0.00	Students loans	$1,000.00
Jewelry	$1,000.00	Credit Card debt	$100.00
Household Items	$1,000.00	Other loans	$0.00
Retirement accounts	$1,000.00		
Bonds	$1,000.00		
Stocks	$1,000.00		
Mutual Funds	$1,000.00		
Cash Value of Life Insurance	$1,000.00		
Savings Bonds			
Checking and savings	$1,000.00		
Cash	$1,000.00		
Other			
Total Assets	**$12,000.00**	**Total Liabilities**	**$3,100.00**

The site creates a small report showing a current net worth of $8,900. Remember the net worth is total assets, in this case $12,000 minus the total liabilities which is $3,100, resulting in a net worth of $8,900. This is important to know as you're mapping out your plans.

Bankrate.com also gave me a quick report showing that if assets grew by a system default of 7%, and my liabilities changed at system default rate of 0%, the net worth after 10 years would be $18,962. I would not rely on this projection because it is too simplistic. But it does give you a great starting place. Websites like this are good for creating what if scenarios. I used this same site to remove all none investments and set the return to 7% and debt to 1% increase. Using the new numbers, the system created a tailored forecast for projected net worth.

Assets		Liabilities	
Home	$0.00	Home mortgage principal	$0.00
Other real-estate	$0.00	Other mortgage principal	$0.00
Automobiles	$0.00	Auto loans	$0.00
Other vehicles	$0.00	Students loans	$1,000.00
Jewelry	$0.00	Credit Card debt	$100.00
Household Items	$0.00	Other loans	$0.00
Retirement accounts	$1,000.00		
Bonds	$1,000.00		
Stocks	$1,000.00		
Mutual Funds	$1,000.00		
Cash Value of Life Insurance	$1,000.00		
Savings Bonds	$0.00		
Checking and savings	$0.00		
Cash	$0.00		
Other			
Total Assets	**$5,000.00**	**Total Liabilities**	**$1,100.00**

The new current net worth is $3,900. Assets totaled $5,000 and $1,100 was the total for liabilities. If the assets were to grow at an annual rate of 7% and the liabilities change at an annual rate of 1% the net worth after 10 years would be $7,989. By adjusting the annual rate of return and increasing the annual rate of liabilities you are able to create a benchmark to use for your investment accounts.

Once all your paperwork is gathered the net worth calculations can be done in minutes. Keep in mind this is not busy work. All the documents you're pulling together will be used in your estate-planning phase.

Determining Your New Net Worth

Everyone creates his or her net worth either by doing something or by not doing anything. What you own and what you owe is constantly changing. By taking a step back and looking at your natural net worth you can now plan for your new natural net worth. Taking charge of our net worth is part of our enhanced Christian life; part of the abundant life that you were promised. Your steps for creating your new net worth are simple.

1. Meditate on God's word. It's always best to start with the word. I would start with a simple principle that I should have a net worth.

John 10:10 AMP
The thief comes only in order to steal and kill and destroy. I came that they may have and enjoy life, and have it in abundance [to the full, till it overflows].

Don't over complicate this step. In your quiet time just ask, "Lord where do you want my net worth to be, what are my goals?" Be prepared for a big answer. (Ephesians 3:20) says God is able to do exceeding, abundantly above all that we ask or think.

2. Set some goals. Allow God to help you in setting your goals. In the previous chapter you created your budget goal, now it's time to expand those goals. The first time you do this exercise you may come back saying, "I have no goals from God". I believe we all have a scripture, a word from God. Before you give up I challenge you to go back through your mind, journal, and notes and look to see if you truly have no goals from God. God is always speaking to us and telling us what he wants for us, but many times because things don't appear as or when we think they should we forget about the promise or desire he gave us. What promise did you let go? What is that dream you wanted that you thought was just too out of reach for you? Is it something as simple as a college degree? A new car for your family? How about a small piece of land you can call your own? These are all goals and until you present it to the Lord how do you know you can't have it?

2 Corinthians 1:20 KJV
For all the promises of God in him are yea, and in him Amen, unto the glory of God by us.

The first time I truly let God set my goals my response was "I can't do all this!" I mean I got a list of goals all out of my reach. I recall three of my larger immediate goals were pay off my house, go back to school, and run a marathon. There was no pay increase. There was no tuition reimbursement. There were no envelopes showing up with checks helping to fund all these activities. My work schedule didn't change allowing me to study and run. I had to go back to God for instructions. I didn't like the instructions. There were times when I complained how unfair it was. While my friends were having late dinners on Friday nights I was home hydrating getting ready for a long run on Saturday. While it seemed everyone was doing all-inclusive vacations I was paying extra payments on my home with no vacation. I had to make a conscious decision to follow the instructions and stand on God's word. I used (Luke 5:5) which says "nevertheless at they word".

Luke 5:5 KJV
And Simon answering said unto him, Master, we have toiled all the night, and have taken nothing: nevertheless at thy word I will let down the net.

I'm pretty sure you're not going to like the instructions either, however the results are well worth it. Remember you only have to follow the instructions and God does the work. (Zechariah 4:6) reminds us that it's "Not by might, nor by power, but by my spirit, saith the Lord of hosts".

Ephesians 3:20-21 MSG
God can do anything, you know–far more than you could ever imagine or guess or request in your wildest dreams! He does it not by pushing us around but by working within us, his Spirit deeply and gently within us.

3. Make your goals visible. Everyone knows Habakkuk 2:2, write the vision and make it plain. There's a good reason for

this. Writing down goals transforms your goals from hopes and dreams to reality.

Habakkuk 2:2-3 KJV
And the LORD answered me, and said, Write the vision, and make it plain upon tables, that he may run that readeth it. For the vision is yet for an appointed time, but at the end it shall speak, and not lie: through it tarry, wait for it; because it will surely come, it will not tarry.

Studies show that people who don't write down their goals tend to fail more than people who do. Dominican University of California's clinical psychologist Dr. Gail Matthews did a study on goal setting. She found that writing down your dreams causes your left and your right brain to function together. Thinking about a goal triggers the right side of your brain known as the imaginative center. By writing down the goal you now trigger the left side of the brain which is logic. When the two sides work together they send signals to your consciousness and every cell in your body. It is believed that by writing down your goals you kindle a new level of thinking, and productivity in your subconscious. You begin to see opportunities that you never saw before.

Writing down your goals forces you to be clear and focused even when resistance comes. In many cases goals will propel you to action and soon you will see your progress. Do not limit yourself. I knew a gentleman who set family goals. He typed up the family goals, laminated the document and gave each member of the family a copy to carry with them. No matter where they were and what they did they knew who they were and where they were going as a family.

Your goals can be written as a prayer. Your goals can be written as affirmations/ confirmations. Often, I will do a combination of the two. I post the affirmations where I need to see them. For example, one day there may be a large piece of paper on the refrigerator that says, "I will eat my veggies first". I intentionally make it large so I cannot ignore it.

Another method I use for visualizing my goals is creating a dream board. Some people call it a vision board. It seems I was doing this before I knew what it was called. When I got my first real apartment I would cut out the things I wanted to buy and post them on the refrigerator. I later found that this was the basis for a dream board.

You can make it as involved or as simple as you like. To accomplish this task, you need to collect images and phases that describe your goals. Most people use magazines to collect what they need. There is no wrong or right way to create the board, you cannot fail at this task. If you're not a magazine person the web is full of examples and places where you can find positive phases and pictures. I tend to create a new one every few years. Also consider adding your picture to the board. I have a friend who added her picture surrounded by all the places she wanted to go. One day while in her office I realized she had gone to 90% of the places listed.

Courtesy of Marisha Telemaque

Next Step

Remember this is not busy work. All the documents you're pulling together are needed for your estate-planning phase. Before moving on to estate planning, apply steps 2 – 5 from the Principles for Life.

#2 Discuss with God (James 5:16, 1 Peter 3:12)
#3 Get Revelation (Word) (James 1:5, Proverbs 4:7, John 14:26)
#4 Receive Instructions (Proverbs 8:33, Proverbs 13:1)
#5 Follow the Instructions (Proverbs 4:13, Proverbs 19:20)

God's promise to you is engrafted; it's attached like a skin graft (James 1:21). Although you have forgotten about it you still have it. That promise is part of you. Hold on to the word given to you by God. Meditate on the word given to you; receive wisdom and understanding. Goals are meant to expand, extend, and grow your perfect self. They are challenging and force you to raise your expectations.

Matthew 5:48 AMPC
You, therefore,, must be perfect [growing into complete maturity of godliness in mind and character, having reached the proper height of virtue and integrity], as your heavenly Father is perfect.

If you're allowing what you own to determine your worth, your math is off.

Chapter 4
Estate Planning

Proverbs 13:22 AMPC
A good man leaves an inheritance [of moral stability and goodness] to his children's children, and the wealth of the sinner [finds its way eventually] into the hands of the righteous, for whom it was laid up.

Definition

If you own anything of value that you would pass on to someone else upon your death, you have an estate. An item does not have to have a large dollar value to be included in your estate plan. In fact, your estate plan should include distribution of personal items such as family photos, artwork, and jewelry.

When you say estate planning most people think of Wills, Trusts, and Estate Taxes. Estate planning is stewardship that covers your latter years as well as when you're no longer here. The stewardship of what you leave on earth when you die is something very few people give serious thought to. It's just as important to God how you distribute what's left of His property, as it is how you manage it while you are alive. Whether you know it or not, you have an estate plan. If you don't get around to writing a will or designing a plan of your own, the state has one for you.

Estate planning starts early not when you're 65 and retired. Discussion with your children and family should be a continual conversation. According to the National Council on Aging, over 25 million Americans aged 60+ are economically insecure - meaning poor. In far too many cases the severity of the situation is unknown thus friends and family don't give assistance. There are numerous stories of adult children reaching out to their parents to discuss the parents' economic situation and being turned away or made to feel like vultures. Having timely financial discussions with your children and family eliminates any awkwardness and misunderstanding in later years.

Estate planning has many steps, here are some documents to consider in your plan:

- ☐ Letter of Intent
- ☐ Beneficiary Designations
- ☐ Durable Power of Attorney
- ☐ Healthcare Power of Attorney
- ☐ Last Will and Testament
- ☐ Living Trusts
- ☐ Guardianship Designations

Letter of Intent

A Letter of Intent is a "blueprint" for other estate planning documents. You simply leave this document to your executor or to your beneficiary. A Letter of Intent is most helpful for those details not included in your legal documents (ex. will, trust or power of attorney) details such as funeral arrangements, care regarding your pets, guardianship of minor children, and special requests. Although this document may not necessarily be valid in the eyes of the law, it helps inform a probate judge of your intentions and may help in the distribution of your assets if the will is deemed invalid. A letter of intent is a living document so add to it and remove things as you see fit.

Beneficiary Designations

Many possessions can pass to your heirs without being dictated in the will, such as 401(k), insurance plans, and retirement accounts. It is important to update your beneficiary (and a contingent beneficiary) on your accounts. Make certain that all beneficiaries you name are over the age of 21 and are mentally competent. Most minor children lack the experience needed to handle a large sum of money; by law minors cannot manage an inheritance without an adult overseeing the assets until they reach the age of maturity in their state. In short, the guardian of the child has access to the funds until the child is legally an adult.

If you don't name a beneficiary or if the beneficiary is deceased or unable to serve, it will be left up to the courts to decide the fate of your funds.

Durable Power Of Attorney (POA)

Your estate plan should include end of life issues such as incapacity. With a durable power of attorney, you assign an agent or a person to act on your behalf in the event of your disability. Without a power of attorney, it may be left to the courts to decide what happens to your assets (if you are found to be mentally incompetent). There is no guarantee the court's decision will be what you wanted.

The Durable Power of Attorney will give your agent the power to enter into financial transactions and make other legal decisions as if he or she were you. This type of Power of Attorney (POA) is revocable by you at any time, typically a time when you are deemed to be physically able, deemed mentally competent or upon death.

It's common for spouses to set up powers of attorney naming the other spouse. Before doing this, make sure it makes sense. In some cases, it may make more sense to name another family member, friend or trusted advisor who is more financially knowledgeable.

Healthcare Power of Attorney (POA)

Like the durable power of attorney, you will assign another individual to make important healthcare decisions on your behalf in the event you are incapacitated. It is important to pick someone whom you trust, who shares your views and who would likely recommend a course of action that you would agree with. This person may literally have to make a life and death decision for you. In case your initial pick is unavailable or unable to act at the time needed a backup person should also be identified.

Last Will and Testament

A Steward makes sure that assets entrusted to him or her are transferred at death with as little confusion, complexity and delay as possible. A will should be one of the main components of the estate plan regardless of the size of the estate. A will states your final wishes. It's one of the legal documents crafted from the Letter of Intent. A lawyer should construct this document. As believers, you should pray regarding with whom to leave your belongings.

Proverbs 20:21 NLT
An inheritance obtained too early in life is not a blessing in the end

Your will should be written so it is consistent with those assets that pass outside the will such as retirement accounts and insurance policies. Naming a different person in the will than the person named as beneficiary on a policy may cause one of the parties to contest your will.

Remember not having a will does not mean nothing is done. It means that your heirs must now go through the court system and the rules on who gets what may not be what you intended. Dying without a will means your estate is at the mercy of the state intestacy succession laws. For blended families, this can mean that a child you raised and whom you cared for has no rights and will inherit nothing. In many states, the order of succession is spouse, child, parent, brother or sister. Stepchildren are not included.

Living Trusts

A living trust can be tricky and it is not for everyone. Think of a trust as a manual on how your assets should be handled in your later years and upon death. Because this is a legal document I would suggest you discuss the matter with a qualified legal person, perhaps an estate-planning attorney. This will ensure the document is done properly in accordance to your state. You also want to make sure the document meets all of your objectives.

A living trust can be revocable or irrevocable. When creating a revocable living trust a trustee must be named. Individuals or couples typically name themselves as the trustee or co-trustee. This allows them the ability to control and benefit from the assets for the rest of their lives. If constructed properly the trust can provide stability from the time when both spouses are living until the death of the surviving spouse.

At the time the trust is created, a successor trustee should be named. This allows for smooth transition in the event the original trustee becomes incapacitated. With a revocable living trust the grantor, creator of the trust retains the ability to revise the trust up until death.

The other type of living trust is irrevocable living trust. With an irrevocable trust you permanently give away your assets during your lifetime. Once given away you do not have control of these assets. These assets are no longer part of your estate and aren't subject to estate taxes. Research shows that irrevocable trusts are rare for most people. It assumes you have more money than you or a spouse could ever use.

There are a lot of reasons for creating a living trust. Some reasons are:

1. **No Probate** – Trusts do not go through probate so assets can be distributed quickly. Normally a trust estate can be settled quicker than a probate estate.

2. **Revocable** – Revocable Living Trust can be changed at any time by the grantor.

3. **Privacy** – Assets can be transferred without being part of the courts' public records.

4. **Separation of Assets** – This is useful for married couples with assets acquired before the marriage. Perhaps there is a family home passed down before the marriage that the spouse would like to leave to a niece or nephew. This can be stipulated in the trust.

5. **Control guardianship spending** – A living trust can dictate how much is given to minor children by the guardian. For example, you can name the trust as beneficiary on an insurance policy then through the trust you can specify how and when you want the money to be distributed to the heir, the minor child.

A living trust is an approach that may work from some. It is not a silver bullet that will solve all your issues and it does not replace a will. Cost can vary so be clear on your objectives and get proper assistance.

Guardianship Designations

I can't think of a more important yet often overlooked task. Selecting a guardian for minor children is a necessity. Your child's very existence is at stake. You should not make this decision without prayer. At a minimum, the individual or couple you choose should share your views, is financially sound and genuinely willing to raise children. A grandparent is not always the best choice. As with all designations, a backup or contingent individual/family should be named as well.

Have discussions with your chosen guardian. Yes they love your child; however, they may need time to wrap their mind around the idea and perhaps prepare themselves and their family. Who will care for your children should not be a surprise if you pass away. You should make it official and include guardianship in your will.

Critical Mishaps When Estate Planning

Before you dive headlong into estate planning be mindful of some typical missteps. Here are a few common problems I see when people develop their estate plan.

1. **Time** – Often people give up before they're done. Estate planning takes time. If you've done your budget and net worth you have the majority of the information required to move forward. Keep in mind there's no reason everything needs to be completed in a day or a week. It took you a long time to accumulate your assets so you should allow yourself time to determine what you want done. In some cases, these are life and death decision so don't rush.

   Remember things change so you need to change your estate plan to match. Just get started and let it unfold.

2. **Leaving your family out of the discussion** – Too often we leave the discussion around finances and estate planning to the end of our lives. By that time it can be overwhelming and a very awkward discussion. Sometimes due to incapacity people simply run out of time and their family is left with making life decisions without expressly knowing what the person wanted. People send out little snippets such as, "My brother Mike loves my car; I'm leaving it to him and you know my sister Sue needs a home". This is not estate planning and it is not constructive. Often this approach leads

to hurt feelings, fractured relationships, and family discord. In the end, it may lead to a legal power struggle that you never intended, where the only happy people are the lawyers. The sooner you start these discussions the better. Here are some suggestions on how to approach the topic.

- ☐ **Use stories** – Someone you knew who didn't have a plan and how it worked out, sort of a cautionary tale. This approach lets your family and friends know you have a plan or at least you're thinking about it.

- ☐ **Get help from others** – This can be very helpful when discussing finances with a parent or a sibling. It's okay to bring in a financial advisor. Let your family hear what you're hearing so you're all on the same page. While visiting my grandparents I saw more insurance agents than I could count. But I knew what policies they had and where they were kept. This made me knowledgeable when it came time to purchase my own insurance. I knew the terms and had some understanding on the process.

- ☐ **Discuss your future** – Tell your family about your retirement plans. Do you plan to travel? Do you have a will? What's your plan in the event you're incapacitated?

No matter which method you decide realize you are not losing power. It's okay to be clear you're not looking for someone to take over your finances. Your point is to educate your friends and family on your life decisions. This is a great way to inform your family of any financial shortfalls you see coming down the road. Most adult children understand they may need to contribute financially to help their parents at some time in life. Letting the children know early allows them to assist the parent with either fortifying the parent's plan or incorporating the parent into their plan. Having these discussions lets everyone strategize without stressing out at the last minute.

1 Timothy 5:4 AMPC
But if a widow has children or grandchildren, see to it that these are first made to understand that it is their religious duty [to defray their natural obligation to those] at home, and make return to their parents or grandparents [for all their care by contributing to their maintenance], for this is acceptable in the sight of God.

3. **Not making a plan** – This is probably the most common mistake that seems to affect every socioeconomic group. We constantly hear of friends and family as well as the very wealthy who die intestate. The news of families fighting it out makes for good television but not when it's your family. This is an avoidable problem. Start with your letter of intent, the blueprint for your other documents.

4. **Poor record keeping** – As my grandparents would say, "Where are the papers"? In 2016, Lesley Stahl from *60 Minutes* reported how some life insurance companies didn't pay benefits even when they knew the policyholder was dead. Twenty-five of the nation's biggest life insurance companies agreed to pay more than $7.5 billion in back-death benefits. The beneficiaries either didn't know there was a policy or couldn't find it to make a claim to the proper insurance company. Having to spend hours organizing and tracking down assets without your assistance is a barrier to moving forward with your estate plans.

Your estate should include an estate planning workbook. The document outlines all your activities and where everything is located. Your executor will use this concise document to ensure things are done according to your wishes.

There is no need to recreate the wheel to generate the estate planning workbook. You can start by using your net worth document.

Asset	Debt
Real Estate	Mortgages
Home, Rental Property, Second Home, Other	Home mortgage payoff, Equity Credit Line, Other
Investments	**Personal Loans**
Stocks, Bonds, Savings Bonds, Retirement Account, Savings, CD, Mutual Funds, Cash Value of Life Insurance Policy	Car Loan, Personal Loans, Student Loans, Life Insurance Loans, Other
Personal Property	**Credit Cards**
Car, RV, Jewelry, Boat, Household Items, Other Luxury Goods	Credit Cards, Other Installment Loans
Cash	
Checking, Savings, Cash, Money Market, Other	

Expand this list to include key contacts such as doctors, attorney, personal information such as birth certificates, driver's license, military discharge papers and your estate plan documents - wills, trust and letter of intent. Don't forget to include any online access along with log in IDs and passwords. It's up to you if you wish to review this document with your executor or if you simply decide to make them aware it exists. Make sure they know where the document is and how they can gain access. If you've stored the document electronically and secured it with a password your executor will need to know your password.

There are numerous options to assist you in pulling this information together. Years ago I found a PDF on the web called "Organizing your financial life – Merrill Lynch". I found this to be very comprehensive. There are a lot of choices out there to get you started, just do a web search on "estate planning workbook".

5. **No beneficiary** –This problem can be immediately resolved and very important for pay-on-death accounts which pass directly to beneficiaries such as bank accounts, retirement, and life insurance policies. Failure to name beneficiaries can result in no one receiving your assets or having the state determine who receives your assets. Review

your accounts to ensure that those to whom you intended to leave your assets are clearly documented.

6. **Not incorporating your Christian values** - Your estate plan should represent who you are as a Christian. This may go against generally accepted guidelines but God's wishes should govern who should receive your assets.

   Some people elect to include their local church when deciding which organizations to include in their trust. Most churches have rules when receiving donations. For example, I found many churches ask that you not donate when you have minor children dependent on the funds. They advise that once the children have been educated and perhaps helped into their first homes to whatever extent the parents choose, then and only then it's okay to donate. Check with your local church for directions. Don't separate your beliefs from your planning.

Next Step
For ease of use, start with your letter of intent and estate planning workbook.

Don't allow fear to hinder you in creating a peaceful transition for your family.

Chapter 5
Retirement

Psalm 128:1-2 KJV
Blessed is every one that feareth the Lord; that walketh in his ways. For thou shalt eat the labour of thine hands: happy shalt thou be, and it shall be well with thee.

Definition

Retirement can be defined as the termination of an individual's work career at a certain age with the expectation that he or she will no longer undertake paid employment.

In Chapter 2 allocation of funds were discussed:

1. Giving Tithes and Offering – Kingdom Business
2. Personal Responsibility - Pay your bills
3. Long Term Goals – (here's where you invest) Education, Retirement, Car, Home
4. Me Time (you're last)

Retirement is third on the list and I hear people pray over and over again Psalms 91. They declare verse 16 "With long life will I satisfy him, and shew him my salvation". However, they fail to plan for the long life they prayed for. People take care of other goals such as cars, homes even education but neglect to prepare for emergencies and retirement. I'm hearing of more emergency funds but lack luster retirement planning.

Like estate planning, more and more people are putting off retirement planning to their later years. Many people function under the time value of money (TVM) principle. In short, their belief is that money currently available is worth more than the same money in the future due to earning capacity. Meaning most people would rather have $10,000 now rather than later. The problem with this theory is you'll never have enough for retirement if you spend it now. They also neglect to take into account interest earned on future money. Even TVM takes into consideration interest. Here's how it works - if you took $10,000 and invested it at an annual rate of 4.99% the future value at the end of the first year would be $10,499. If you kept that same $10,000 at 4.99% for 10 years your future value would be $15,529.69.

Year		Additions	Interest	Balance
Start		$10,000.00		$10,000.00
	1	$0.00	$449.99	$10,449.99
	2	$0.00	$470.25	$10,920.24
	3	$0.00	$491.40	$11,411.64
	4	$0.00	$513.52	$11,925.16
	5	$0.00	$536.63	$12,461.79
	6	$0.00	$560.77	$13,022.56
	7	$0.00	$586.01	$13,608.57
	8	$0.00	$612.39	$14,220.96
	9	$0.00	$639.94	$14,860.90
	10	$0.00	$668.74	$15,529.64

By putting off retirement planning you lose the opportunity and benefit of time to grow your retirement accounts.

What the Bible Says About Retirement

In my research, I have found only one scripture which speaks of retirement as we know it that is Numbers 8:24-26. Here it speaks of the Levites and their work in the tabernacles. According to scripture, service in the tabernacle was from age 25-50 years old and after 50 they retired from regular service. After the age of 50 they could assist but no physical or challenging work.

Numbers 8:24-26 AMP
This is what applies to the Levites: from twenty-five years old and upward they shall enter to perform service in the work of the Tent of Meeting, but at the age of fifty years, they shall retire from the service of the [tabernacle] work and serve no longer. They may assist their *brothers in the Tent of Meeting* to keep an obligation, but they shall do no [heavy or difficult] work. thus deal with the Levites concerning their obligations.

What Should Retirement Look Like?

I do not believe there is a set time for a Christian to retire from their job or career as outlined in our culture. I believe like your net worth a Christian has the power and authority through Christ to define their retirement date. Neither your job nor the government can decide the day and year you retire.

Many people can't wait to retire simply because they want to leave their job. It's like a prison sentence. People feel like they've gotten a sentence of 15 to life. They look at retirement as a time to sit and rest. They fail to plan past rest. Too many people are becoming stationary. Inactivity often leads to disability; this is not part of the abundant life Christ promised the believer. I cannot find an example of inactivity in the Bible. If you research Joshua 13:1, you find he was between 90 and 100 years old, however he still has a purpose and an assignment from God. That lets you know he was active. I'm all for rest but I'm not for idleness.

Retirement Planning

Once you understand you determine your retirement you'll see why common rules of thumbs wouldn't work for you. There are a lot of philosophies surrounding retirement planning. I hear people say they need one million dollars to retire. I'm not sure where this number came from but let's do some simple math. If you retire at age 50 and live until 90 that's 40 years. If we calculate a 2.29% return (10 yr. Treasury Rate), you would have to live off of $3,178 a month with a balance of $78.71 in year 40. On face value this sounds like a plan, however the idea that you're going to have the same lifestyle from age 50 to 90 is unrealistic.

One theory discussed a lot is the rule of 4%. The rule is based on a study done by financial planner William Bengen. Bengen found that 4% was the highest rate that held up under a period of at least 30 years. It works this way - you can safely withdraw 4% of your retirement savings each year without running out of money.

There are several problems with these simple plans. Many plans simply look at current spending then attempt to figure out how much is needed in order to sustain that level of living in the future. Most people intend to have completely different spending patterns in retirement than they did during their careers. With a simple plan, there is no adjustment for inflation. The plans do not take into consideration any 'what if' scenarios. Do you have an aging parent that needs your financial help? Do you have a child in college or a child back in your home that you support? Are you traveling? Do you have a mortgage? Do you require long-term care?

You must also consider the year you retire. If done later in life you could run into an adjustment needed year 70 ½ to satisfy the IRS's required minimum distribution (RMD) for 401(k)s, IRAs and similar accounts. In short, the IRS has a life expectancy table they use and update to determine how much should be withdrawn from retirement accounts. If you fail to take out the minimum after age 70 you will be penalized.

To start your retirement planning you need to work the first Principle for Life (determine the problem). You need to ask yourself some questions around retirement:

- ☐ What are you going to do?
- ☐ Where are you going to live?
- ☐ Are you going to travel?
- ☐ Do you need two homes?
- ☐ Are you going to take classes? Learn a new language, play an instrument, get a degree?
- ☐ Are you going to the mission field? Who's taking care of your home while you're away?
- ☐ How much does all this cost?

Document what your dreams and desires are for retirement. Remember it's important to write out all your goals. Before you determine if you can afford it, pray about it. Pray again? Yes, pray again!

1 Peter 3:12 KJV
For the eyes of the Lord are over the righteous, and his ears are open unto their prayers: but the face of the Lord is against them that do evil.

When I first started thinking of retirement, I pictured a home in the Caribbean somewhere in the hills with a small garden to grow vegetables. With some careful planning this was an achievable goal so I took my thoughts and ideas to God and his response was "think bigger". Remember goals are meant to expand, extend and grow you. I now have a retirement plan that is different and bigger. Now I have a retirement plan, which God has to do, my job is to follow the instructions and expand, extend and grow.

Once you've confirmed with God what retirement looks like for you, next you can work out a plan to get there. Figure out how much does all this cost. Your net worth document and estate planning workbook illustrates exactly where you stand financially and through prayer you know where you're going. There are many retirement calculators that determine how much you need and allow for 'what if' scenarios at various rate of return.

Here's something I created using data found on the web using averages - age (50), income (50,000), and retirement savings ($250,000). Remember these calculators are adjustable so you can see how small changes yield big results.

Keep saving. Adjust the numbers below to see how they may affect your score.

Remember, your score is based on planning until age 93 in the underperforming market, so it represents a conservative estimate of how much income you could have during retirement.

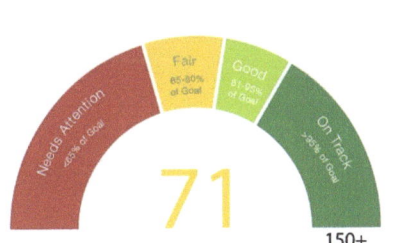

We think you'll need about

$3,952

PER MONTH IN RETIREMENT

_____

You could have about

$2,816

PER MONTH IN RETIREMENT
including $1,285 from Social Security

About you: Current age: 50 | Annual income: $50K | Current savings: $250K | Planning age: 93

Get Your Financial House In Order, 2nd Edition

When planning for retirement, be prepared to work strategically and don't forget to use The Principles for Life:

- ☐ **Determine the problem** - You worked out the numbers of what you have and what you need.

- ☐ **Discuss with God** - In prayer discuss with God the issue and what you see your part as. Take all your ideas and solutions to God for approval.

- ☐ **Get Revelation (Word)** –Allow God to speak to you during prayer and through his word.

- ☐ **Receive Instructions** – Like revelation instructions can come in different ways. I always take a pen and paper with me when I pray. So as ideas and impressions come I can write them down.

- ☐ **Follow the Instructions** – I can't express how important this step is. You may not like the instructions but follow the instructions.

Strategically you want to go ahead and fine-tune your savings, investments and retirement plan. Get creative and find the money you need. Start simple and start using some of the familiar savings strategies you've heard of. For example, live off of your pre-raise income. If you get a raise at work, instead of figuring that money into your budget allocate it to retirement. Tax your bad habits. Can't get enough of fast food or junk food? Tax yourself every time you purchase that bad habit item. Better yet, give up your bad habit and reward yourself. Start giving up your bad habits and place the money you would have spent into the retirement account.

Do your investment homework. Brush up on your investment knowledge. Do now show up at the financial planners' office or brokers' office with a big pile of money. There are a lot of investment options available, but they all start with you. All investments involve some degree of risk. You need to have an idea what your risk tolerance is. Risk and reward go hand in hand, so understanding the amount of risk you are comfortable with is important. Many investment websites offer free online questionnaires to help you assess your level of risk. Keep in mind that any investment suggestions may be biased toward the site's financial products or services.

Know your investment horizon. That's a fancy way of saying know the amount of time the investment can sit without being touched. How many years do you have before you leave your employment and retire?

Once you have identified your risk tolerance and your investment horizon, you can pick the proper investment. Stay true to yourself. If you determine you have a low risk tolerance do not allow yourself to be talked into something speculative. Also, if you cannot explain it you should not invest in it. You must be comfortable with what you're doing.

Proverbs 10:4 NLT
Lazy people are soon poor; hard words get rich.

Does Retirement Planning Take Time?
Absolutely! But you have the majority of the information already. If you did a vision board (dream board) your retirement should already be on there; you simply need to give it legs. If you did a budget and net worth document you have a clear picture of your financial state. You know how much you need vs. what you have. Simply apply steps 2 -5 of the Principles for Life.

Is It Too Late to Plan for Retirement?
I don't believe it's ever too late to improve your life. Time is a big factor when creating a retirement plan. Investing over long periods of time is a sure way of increasing your net worth. Setting aside a small amount of money each month improves your financial stability.

Your savings could be worth $6441.96 after 10 years.
If you save $50.00 per month your savings may grow to $6,441.96 after 10 years. This includes a starting balance of $1.00 and a 1.4% annual rate of return.

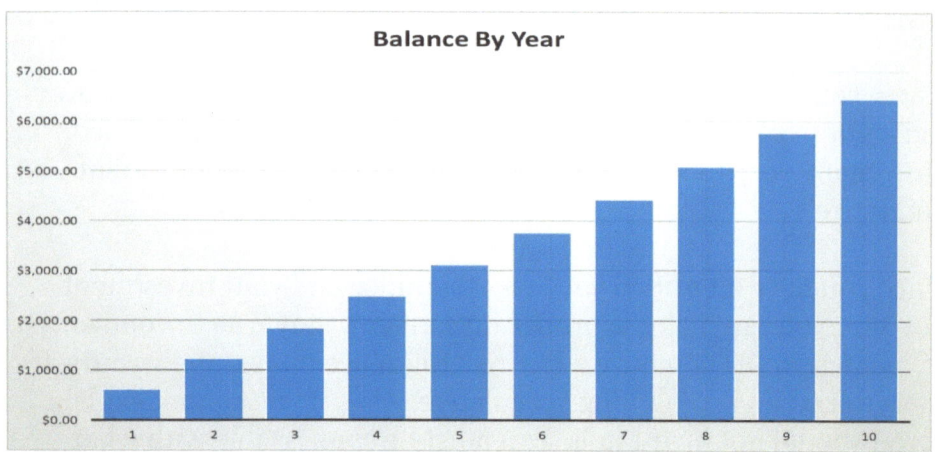

If your time is limited your approach will have to change to reflect that. I believe your late start is like the parable of the vineyard workers (Matthew 20:15). In short although people started working at different times they all received the same pay. What stood out for me was verse 20.

Matthew 20:15 AMPC
Am I not permitted to do what I choose with what is mine? [Or do you begrudge my being generous?] Is your eye evil because I am good?

God can do what he wishes with what is his and that includes your retirement.

Next Step
Determine what retirement should look like. Be prepared to take action and think strategically.

Like net worth, you get to determine what retirement from your job looks like.

Chapter 6
Epilogue

Proverbs 21:5 NLT
Good planning and hard work lead to prosperity, but hasty shortcuts lead to poverty.

When I teach I give my bio like most people but when I think about what qualifies me to teach on financial matters I like what one author said in response to the question - stupid mistakes were his major accomplishment. I found that to be so true. Making rash and stupid mistakes but later being open to God to assist me in fixing the problem made me a prime candidate for this work. People ask if I teach non-believers. Of course, the wisdom of God works no matter what.

For some reason people think financial people never make financial mistakes. The only difference between you and the so-called financial guru is the guru knows they're wrong while they're making poor decisions. Financial people neglect to make wills, although we tell everyone else to do it right away. Even I have failed to follow the Principles for Life a few times. When looking for my last car purchase I got so wrapped up in the process I took on someone else's image for the vehicle. Before I realized it my must have items included seat warmers, sunroof, and a high-tech computer system. I went as far as to pick out a car and hadn't discussed it with God; I hadn't received a revelation nor instructions. Finally, I applied the "Principles for Life" and prayed about it only to realize I didn't care about any of that stuff on my must have list. I really cared about mileage and trunk space. I had taken what someone else considered must haves and made them my own.

Even teaching and writing was a struggle. It actually took three prophets I trusted to look me in the eye and say "teach". God allowed me to start small by teaching at a small loving church. So if you've been beating yourself up for not making the right decisions, stop it. We all make mistakes. Beating yourself up is unproductive. Now is a great time to change so you can live the life God intended you to live.

Principles for Life

"The Principles for Life" are not new. You may have seen them packaged in a different way. As I went through life I kept finding that I used the same steps over and over when faced with issues. I found the principles always work when I apply them and thus I have included them in this book. Below are the steps with a few scriptures I often use.

- ☐ Understand the Problem – (Psalm 49:20, Psalms 32:9)
- ☐ Discuss with God - (James 5:16, 1 Peter 3:12)
- ☐ Get Revelation (Word) (James 1:5, Proverbs 4:7)
- ☐ Receive Instructions - (Psalm 37:23, Proverbs 19:20, Proverbs 13:1)
- ☐ Follow the Instructions - (Proverbs 4:13, Proverbs 19:20, Proverbs 8:33)

If you forget everything written in this book but hold on to these five steps you'll still be ahead of most people.

I know that to complete all the task in this book will take time. I hear people say all the time "I have a concern now". Heck I've even said it. But God's answer to me is the answer I give you, take action now! Now is the time to get out of the natural, the world's way of doing things, and into God's way of doing things. When you're broke in the natural, you hoard. But in the kingdom, you give. If you want supernatural increase you can't leave out God.

Once you release your situation to God you will find his way is faster, multi-layered, structured, and permanent. We often have cares that bind and inhibit. Several years ago, God taught me the meaning of 'casting your cares'.

1 Peter 5:7 AMP
Casting all your cares [all your anxieties, all your worries, and all your concerns, once and for all] on Him, for He cares about you [with deepest affection, and watches over you very carefully.

To cast means to cause to move, to throw or set forth. God revealed to me that a care is like garbage, it's useless. He said I should visualize myself taking that care - worry or anxiety and place it in a plastic garbage bag and throw it over a fence into a garbage dump. Before the garbage man collects the garbage what we often do is go and grab the garbage bag out of the can and stockpile it back into our homes and lives. You know too much garbage (cares, anxieties, worries and concerns) in your home is toxic. Cast away your cares on God for he cares about you with deepest affection, and he watches over you.

About the Author

Psalm 139:23 AMP
Search me [thoroughly], O God, and know my heart; Test me and know my anxious thoughts;

Darlene Rivers, PMP, MBA
Rivers and Assoc. Inc.

BA – Finance, Northern Illinois University
MBA – Lake Forest Graduate School of Management

PMP Certified with 12 plus years of experience.

Author: Get Your financial House In Order

- ☐ My assignment is to counsel and teach financial principles based on the word of God. To give the body of Christ biblical foundation for their finances.

- ☐ My goal is to share how you apply the word of God to your finances with practical tools and application.

- ☐ My desire is to assist all believers in removing the burden of debt and the oppression that accompanies it.

Share your feedback and questions with me at:
riversandassoc.com

Follow me on Facebook:
https://www.facebook.com/riversandassocinc/

Follow me on Twitter:
@RiversandAssoc
https://twitter.com/RiversandAssoc

Resources

Specific resources listed in this book have no connection with the author of the book. They are mentioned as examples. Names and links are provided so the readers may obtain information for themselves. The names and links are subject to change.

Unless otherwise indicated, all Scripture quotations are taken from the Holy Bible, King James Version Public Domain.

King James Version (KJV)
Public Domain

New Living Translation (NLT)
Holy Bible, New Living Translation, copyright © 1996, 2004, 2015 by Tyndale House Foundation. Used by permission of Tyndale House Publishers Inc., Carol Stream, Illinois 60188. All rights reserved.

Amplified Bible (AMP)
Copyright © 2015 by The Lockman Foundation, La Habra, CA 90631. All rights reserved.

Amplified Bible, Classic Edition (AMPC)
Copyright © 1954, 1958, 1962, 1964, 1965, 1987 by The Lockman Foundation

The Message (MSG)
Copyright © 1993, 1994, 1995, 1996, 2000, 2001, 2002 by Eugene H. Peterson

Living Bible (TLB)
The Living Bible copyright © 1971 by Tyndale House Foundation. Used by permission of Tyndale House Publishers Inc., Carol Stream, Illinois 60188. All rights reserved.

New International Version (NIV)
Holy Bible, New International Version®, NIV® Copyright ©1973, 1978, 1984, 2011 by Biblica, Inc.® Used by permission. All rights reserved worldwide.

Rick Warren - Financial Fitness A 21 Day Devotional
https://www.Bible.com/reading-plans/1427-financial-fitness
This devotional © 2014 by Rick Warren. All rights reserved. Used by permission.

Dave Ramsey's Financial Wisdom from Proverbs Devotional – YouVersion
https://www.Bible.com/reading-plans/463-dave-ramsey-proverbs

Bankrate.com Net worth calculator:
http://www.bankrate.com/calculators/smart-spending/personal-net-worth-calculator.aspx#ixzz4cFw0QNMk

The Power of Writing Down Your Goals and Dreams
http://www.huffingtonpost.com/marymorrissey/the-power-of-writing-down_b_12002348.html

The Research: Written Goals Increase Achievement Success -
http://www.goalband.co.uk/the-research.html#sthash.OVF0KD0s.mpKAtqDI.dpuf

6 surprising facts about a living revocable trust
http://www.bankrate.com/finance/estate-planning/living-revocable-trust-facts-1.aspx#ixzz4druKTEl3

Establishing A Revocable Living Trust
http://www.investopedia.com/articles/pf/06/revocablelivingtrust.asp#ixzz4cjFieC5j

Organizing your financial life - Merrill Lynch Login
https://olui2.fs.ml.com/publish/content/.../pdf/.../essential_documents_-_321732pm.pdf L-08-11 @2011 Bank of America Corporation. All rights reserved.

60 Minutes Life insurance industry under investigation
http://www.cbsnews.com/news/60-minutes-life-insurance-investigation-lesley-stahl/

Compound Interest Calculator - Savings Account Interest Calculator
http://www.bankrate.com/calculators/savings/compound-savings-calculator-tool.aspx#ixzz4drvNcg0W

The Fidelity Retirement ScoreSM
https://communications.fidelity.com/pi/2015/retirement/

Budgeting: Utilizing Percentage Benchmarks
http://thedime.copera.org/2013/05/02/budgeting-utilizing-percentage-benchmarks

How to Budget Your Money With the 50/20/30 Guideline
https://www.learnvest.com/knowledge-center/your-ultimate-budget-guideline-the-502030-rule/

My Debt Free Budget Breakdown
https://www.growingslower.com/debt-free-budget-percentage-breakdown/

How to Determine Budget Percentages
https://www.everydollar.com/blog/budget-percentages

Should you follow the 4% retirement rule?
http://money.cnn.com/2016/04/20/retirement/retirement-4-rule/

Assessing Your Risk Tolerance
https://investor.gov/research-before-you-invest/research/assessing-your-risk-tolerance

www.ingramcontent.com/pod-product-compliance
Lightning Source LLC
Chambersburg PA
CBHW041105180526
45172CB00001B/109